Vegan: Essential Beginners Guide to the Vegan Diet and Weight Loss

Tone up, Slim Down and Feel Happy Now

Table of Contents

Introduction

I want to thank you and congratulate you for downloading my book, *"Vegan: Essential Beginners Guide to the Vegan Diet and Weight Loss"*.

Writing this book really was a labor of love for me. I became vegan three years ago when I watched a documentary called Earthlings. Being an animal lover, after watching that documentary I just couldn't bring myself to support an industry like that. Since then I've been so passionate about giving this diet my all. At first, it wasn't easy and I had many struggles. I had no idea that there were that many products that had an animal component in them, nor the amount of food that I thought was vegan but actually wasn't (I'm looking at you bagels!).

Regardless, I persisted and was rewarded. I lost a lot of weight just in the first few months, I started going to the gym encouraged by my progress just from the diet alone. I noticed I looked better and more youthful. I really was seeing results! The reason was I put a lot of time into doing research about how to implement habits, how to overcome cravings and how exactly the weight loss process occurs. Now I'm bringing you this book, with the hopes that I can speed the vegan journey up for you!

The vegan diet really is wonderful. Not only are you becoming more healthy, but you're saving animal lives at the same time – I don't think it could get any better.

Thanks again for downloading this book, I hope you enjoy it!

I would encourage you to share this book with all your friends and family so that we can spread the Vegan love and make this movement even bigger! If you enjoy this book, please leave an honest review. Your feedback means the world to me, and I really hope this book is the beginning of a new you and a healthier, more productive and happier lifestyle.

Chapter 1 – Everything You Need To Know About Being Vegan

Important Things You Need To Know About Being Vegan.

The Vegan Lifestyle is a way of life that has been in existence way before it was even given its name. The word 'vegan' was coined from the word 'vegetarian', in the year 1944; when a small body of vegetarians broke away from the well known Leicester Vegetarian Society.

A vegetarian might only stay away from eating certain animal products, vegans make it a way of life to stay away from any animal product at all. Whether it's food, clothing, hair products, body products, etc. The word was originally defined as a principle of emancipation of animals from the exploitation of man.

What A Vegan Is and What a Vegan isn't

The concept of being vegan has always been misunderstood, even by some newly vegan people. The perfect definition of a vegan would be 'a person who has made a conscious decision to stay away from anything that involves animals or products derived from animals such as meat, eggs, milk, cheese, some wines, refined white sugar, etc. Due to his or her belief in the freedom of animals to coexist freely without being harmed by people.'

Being Vegan is a growing lifestyle and is currently being adopted by a lot of people worldwide. Statistics have shown that more vegan products are being consumed daily in higher percentages and currently, the fastest growing market of vegan products is China. China currently has a sale growth of 17.2%.

There is also a phenomenon in many Western countries, known as Veganuary, where people go Vegan in the month of January. If you are one of these people, this book includes everything you need to know on how to make sure you stick to your new Vegan diet.

Top Reasons People Choose The Vegan Lifestyle

This is a frequently asked question; a lot of people wonder why anyone in his or her right mind would intentionally choose a lifestyle that will make them stay away from meat and other animal products.

Many people are peripherally aware of the suffering that animals go through on a daily basis, but since they haven't been directly exposed to it, they dismiss the Vegan diet as a fad. That being said, there is actually no single or particular reason on why people go Vegan.

The following is a list of reasons why some choose to go Vegan. You might see your reason below, you might also find a new reason and be further inspired to stick with your vegan diet. It's even possible that you have a completely different reason for going Vegan.

Here are some reasons why people could choose to go vegan:

Health Reasons -

A lot of people seeking to avoid a lifestyle that contributes to disorders and diseases such as heart attacks, type II diabetes and even cancer go Vegan. These people usually go vegan in order to reduce the intake of animal products and the harmful effects they can have on the body.

Most vegan products are plant based and they reduce the risk of these terrible diseases as well as lowering the risk of developing Alzheimer's disease and many others.

A Vegan diet also contributes to weight loss, not only is a plant based diet less calorie dense, but provides the right nutrients to slim down quickly. A Vegan diet lowers cholesterol levels, LDLs and blood pressure - this will make you not only feel great, but look great too. In fact, people on a vegan diet typically have their blood pressure 25-75% lower than a person with an animal product diet. This also puts Vegans at a far lower risk of dementia.

Essentially, a Vegan diet will create a healthy lifestyle without even needing to work out. If you do work out as well though, that can produce some incredible results in terms of both weight loss and health! I will explore some of these benefits further later on in the book.

In addition, a lot of the antibiotics used in the modern animal farming system cause a lot of terrible side effects, and by going Vegan people are avoiding these.

For example, excess oestrogen, which is used in order to make animals more 'plump' to increase the meat industries 'yield', can contribute to weight gain when consumed by humans. In addition, high levels of oestrogen have been linked to gynecomastia (colloqually referred to as 'man boobs') in men.

Ethical Reasons -

Quite a number of people choose to go vegan as a way of life because of the beliefs that are attached with it. Being vegan as a way of life is focused on protecting the life and freedom of animals, considering there are other alternatives available that do not involve taking anything from animals. This is how many people are introduced to Veganism and the prevention of animal cruelty is paramount in being a Vegan.

The meat and dairy industry dominate the landscape, attempting to minimize costs and maximize profits at the expense of animals. It is not that Vegans are suggesting that animals get the same treatment as humans, get their own houses and live luxurious lifestyles - rather what is desired is that animals get equal consideration.

By going Vegan, you are contributing massively to the elimination of animal suffering. Every year, the number of people going Vegan grows, so the Vegan industry grows and more and more alternative products are available to the products the meat industry puts out. This is a cycle of positivity that will hopefully one day eliminate all animal suffering.

For The Protection Of The Environment -

The animal agriculture process requires the use of lots and lots of water, and that means that more water is used for this purpose than for producing, for example, cereal grains.

In fact, the amount of water used on a meat eater is more than double the amount of water that would be used to produce the food that a Vegan eats. You might think that there is an abundance of water in the world, considering that the planet is 70% water, however this is not actually the case in terms of drinkable water. It is estimated that by 2030 the world will only have 60% of the water needed if we do not something about it now.

Some people also go Vegan in order to save the trees, as many trees are being cut down in order to create grazing areas for animals as well as make space for their food production.

One of the main reasons why a lot of people choose the vegan lifestyle is because animal agriculture is said to contribute to about 65% of the total of nitrous oxide gas released into the atmosphere and also increase the total amount of methane gas in the atmosphere.

Especially important is the fact that 9% of carbon dioxide emissions globally are said to come from animal agriculture. These are all gases which all play vital roles in air pollution and climate change. So by eliminating the need for animal agriculture, a lot of progress can be made on big issues such as global warming.

To summarize, by going Vegan, you are helping reduce the amount of water being used on animal agriculture so that it can be used by those in need. You are reducing the effect of global climate change and contributing against air pollution. In the next 30 years, if the vegan population keeps growing at the same rate, we'll have made some massive progress towards solving these big issues.

What The Typical Vegan Eats

What do vegans eat? It is true that a lot of societies basic meals contain animal products. Well, what a lot of people don't know about going vegan is that they have a lot of other alternatives to choose from.

Vegans can get creative, as there are actually plenty of foods available for them. In fact, probably more food than you could eat in a lifetime. A typical vegan dish can contain vegetables, tofu, beans, pasta, seeds, nuts, lentils, plant milks, etc, as replacement for animal meals. There are also plant based sweeteners such as stevia instead of refined sugar and honey.

Due to the greater number of Vegan people in the world recently, a lot of shops are now selling ready-made vegan products. You could find ready-made vegan products such as vegan cheese, vegan desserts, as well as vegan meats like tofu in many shops now. As more people become Vegan, this will continue to be the case and the amount of and variety of products will inevitably increase.

The Three Types Of Vegans.

Not all vegans stay away from the same things, or eat the same kinds of foods. The vegan next door can be a different type of vegan to the vegan a few blocks away. There are different types of vegans, these categories are rather broad so you could be a mix of several, but here they are:

Raw Food Vegans -

These types of vegans tend to go for foods that are uncooked. Foods like vegetables, fruits, or other foods that are cooked at very low temperatures.

Junk Food Vegans -

These kinds of vegans rely mostly on processed vegan desserts and foods, like veggie burgers and the sort. Since a lot of Vegan 'junk food' actually tends to be a lot healthier than animal based junk food, this can be a viable diet for weight loss, although it's not recommended to just eat veggie burgers and soya milk ice cream.

Dietary Vegans -

These vegans tend to eat foods that are from a plant based origin. However, dietary vegans may use animal products in other non-edible things like cosmetics, clothes, soaps, shampoos, etc.

This is a route for many beginner Vegans, who do not yet know the extent of animal product use in many items we use in daily life. It is a good starting point and many of these people tend to fully embrace the Vegan lifestyle as time goes on.

Top 10 Things People Tend To Misunderstand About Going Vegan.

1: Being Vegan Is An Unhealthy Lifestyle -

A lot of people tend to think that staying away from animal products equals staying away from a lot of nutrients. However, there are a lot of alternatives to animal products that have the same amount of nutrients or even more. For instance, eating a veggie burger is far healthier than eating a beef burger, due to all the health benefits mentioned before.

Contrary to popular belief, going Vegan does far more good than harm when it comes to your health. There is a plethora of studies to back this up, but I think most people intuitively understand that just by being concerned about what you eat you become healthier, especially when you're eliminating hormone ridden meat products from your diet and replacing them with revitalising plant products.

Society is well aware of the power of plant based cuisine, we have sayings such as 'eat your five a day' and 'an apple a day keeps the doctor away', it's just that many do not take action on these well known platitudes.

2: Being Vegan Is A Hippie Thing Only -

Many people are saddled with the belief that the only people that become vegans are hippies, therefore; it's a hippie thing. Many associate going Vegan with an alternative, holistic lifestyle or that Vegans have a certain doctrine.

But that is a major misconception, as a lot of people from all walks of life are vegans. In fact, one of the major reasons why a lot of people are turning vegan is because a lot of celebrities are ascribing to the lifestyle and these celebrities are role models for many.

In addition, many politicians, doctors, lawyers and teachers all are Vegan and you wouldn't know it by looking at them. Sure, there are the minority of people who telegraph the fact that they are Vegan every chance they have, but this is truly an example of the vocal minority being misrepresented as the majority.

3: Being Vegan Is Unaffordable -

People have the misconception that the vegan lifestyle is very expensive and only people with deep pockets can afford to be vegan. But this is simply not the case.

There are a lot of affordable vegan products that cost you the same amount or even less, when compared to the animal product alternative. It costs you morally less, as well.

A lot of Vegan products such as legumes, nuts and pasta are very affordable and also abundant in food stores. In addition, logically speaking, the less processed the food, the cheaper the healthier it's going to be. Try visiting a market and buying fruit and veg in bulk. You'll be surprised at the kinds of deals you can get.

If you don't feel like visiting the market, many of the popular stores do actually now have online shops, where you can get Vegan products delivered to your door!

4: Going Vegan Makes You Weak -

Another misconception that makes people stay away from the vegan lifestyle is the belief that the vegan body and immune system is somehow weaker than an average person that feeds on animal products.

The image of an iron deficient Vegan pops up into the heads of many. However, being vegan does not in any way make you weak, as vegan products contain all the nutrients that are necessary in order to make your body and immune system strong, actually, eating such a varied diet is a good way to make sure you get even more vitamins, minerals and proteins than a non-vegan, who might just stick to the foods they know and not try anything new.

In fact, there are many successful vegan athletes such as David Meyer in Brazilian Jiu Jitsu whose strength you'd have a hard time denying and Pat Reeves, a female powerlifter who overcame cancer and broke the world deadlift record twice!

5: Going Vegan Is Extremely Hard To Take On -

A lot of people believe that if you are a vegan, it must be difficult, if not impossible to stay away from the animal products that vegans normally stay away from.

This belief that vegans are denying their bodies of what they need discourages a lot of people, thereby, making them stay as far as possible from the possibility of being vegan Of course this isn't true; going vegan is simple once you've made up your mind to take it on and becomes easier the longer you do it for.

Just like anything, with practice and repetition, you will get better. If you put your heart and soul into being Vegan, the results that you get in your personal life will be phenomenal, but also the results that we get together in terms of making the world a better place will be astronomical.

6: Going Vegan Is Boring -

The fact that vegans are required to stay away from certain foods that the majority of the world consume makes people build up the misconception that somehow your dietary options will become too limited; so limited in fact that they make eating or living boring.

This couldn't be further from the truth, once you delve deeply into Vegan cuisine you can tell that there is a plethora of tasty food out there just waiting to be discovered.

It's such an adventure, going vegan allows you to discover food that you didn't even know existed, try new things and even meet new people. Some of the best friends you'll ever make you might meet through vegan circles.

7: The Vegan Diet Is A Kind Of Eating Disorder -

Most people cannot stay away from animal products, and that makes it difficult for them to understand why anyone in their right mind would choose to willingly not eat meat and the likes.

This leads some to interpret it in the only way they know how to, and that is to believe that the people who chose this lifestyle are somehow abnormal and are suffering from a kind of mental illness that manifests itself as an eating disorder.

Evidently, that is the wrong way of looking at things; people that take on the vegan lifestyle have made a conscious decision to live this way, and are perfectly normal for choosing to do this. In fact, after knowing about the kind of suffering that animals experience, how could one not be vegan.

8: The Vegan Lifestyle Is A Dangerous Lifestyle For Kids -

This again brings us back to the fact that there are a lot of vegan alternatives that have even more nutrients in some cases than the average animal product.

Some people think that children that are raised vegans are in some way lacking in nutrients that their counterparts that are raised on animal based products have.

This is not true; children can get the nutrients they require from vegan meals as well. In fact, there are many child vegan athletes who perform extremely well in their respective fields. For example, Cody Elkins was just ten years old when he won the World Outdoor Racquetball championship. He had been Vegan since he was two years old.

9: Vegans Need Supplements -

People tend to think that a typical vegan person needs supplements in order to compensate for his or her 'poor diet', and that is an incorrect notion. As a vegan, you do not need to take supplements, however they can certainly help in the beginning when you're not exactly sure what you are deficient in.

As you are vegan for a longer and longer period of time, you can become familiar with a wider variety of food that will satisfy all nutritional needs so that ideally you don't need any supplements at all. In fact, most people go vegan without any supplementation whatsoever.

10: Going Vegan is a Fad -

Many people think that being a Vegan is becoming a fad or trendy. I would say that, in a sense, that is definitely a good thing. It should be trendy to be saving the planet.

However, in reality, thanks to social media, more people are becoming aware of the cruelty inflicted upon animals and also the health benefits of becoming Vegan.

Call it what you like, there's no denying that being Vegan is one of the best things you can do for your health and unlike fidget spinners, this is a fad I can really get behind.

Vegan Celebrities You Might Not Have Known Were Vegan

A lot of people have taken on the vegan lifestyle due to the fact that various celebrities that they idolize have adopted the vegan lifestyle. There are many celebrities that are currently going vegan, encouraging a lot of people along the way. Some of these celebrities include notable people such as: Ellen DeGeneres, Ariana Grande, Liam Hemsworth, Miley Cyrus, Ellen page, etc.

Most of them chose the vegan lifestyle because they have learnt about the animal cruelty involved in most animal based products. In addition, most of them claimed that becoming Vegan was a great decision on their part and that they don't regret it in any way.

I think it's really great that they're promoting the Vegan diet and lifestyle, and hopefully we can get more celebrity converts in 2018. We've already had WILL.I.AM, looking forward to many more!

Chapter 2 – Vegan Health, Fitness and Mindfulness

How To Go Vegan and the Secret Way Social Media Can Help

It's simple. Just don't eat or use any animal products. Alright alright, you got me. It's not that simple. If you're a vegetarian already, it might be fairly easy for you to switch to being a full vegan, but being truthful, there is a lot of research that needs to be done on how to actually become a vegan. Do I expect you to do what I did and spend countless hours looking for resources online and Googling what foods are vegan? Well, I do expect you to do that last part.

To make it easy for you to get all the right information in, join Vegan groups on Facebook. Join a vegan club at your school or University, follow Vegan instagram accounts, Twitter accounts, maybe even follow Vegan bloggers on tumblr or vloggers on Snapchat.

The more information you have coming in the more likely you are to stick to your diet. If you fully immerse yourself in Vegan culture, your brain is going to slowly realize "Oh wow, we're doing this vegan thing for real then". Then you'll be able to stick to the diet much more easily. This is known as the law of attraction.

Another thing I'd suggest is that before you go to bed every night, write down at the top of a piece of paper "Reasons I'm Going Vegan" and see if you can write at least ten reasons down. What you'll find is, when you get to ten, you'll have way more than that. Keep going and see how many you can write. If you do this every day for a month, I can guarantee that you'll stick to your diet.

The Foolproof Method to Stick To Your Vegan Diet

The jump in method works very well for some people. As you know, when you're trying to get into the water on the beach, what's the most comfortable way to go in? Slowly wade through the water feeling how cold it is on your skin, or jumping in right away?

Well, for some people, they really can't jump in right away. This is why it might be a good idea to go vegetarian for a month and then go fully vegan. This is a perfectly valid method and works wonders if you want to make absolutely sure that you stick to your vegan diet. It also gives you time to research what animal products there are out there and the alternatives to them.

The Mindful Vegan

Meditation and being Vegan are so perfectly synergistic. You can start with just ten minutes a day, sit in a quiet room and try to focus on your breath as it goes in and out. If your attention goes elsewhere, just bring it back to your breath. I find this works best if you have a cushion to sit on, or you can try sitting on a pillow or a chair. You can even do this lying down but be careful not to fall asleep.

Set a little timer, I prefer to use a kitchen timer rather than my phone just because I meditate in the dark and the phone gives off too much light. When the timer buzzes, allow yourself to relax. Now, in this moment of relaxation, think about all the little animal lives you've helped by going vegan. Think about how good your body feels and how you're really making a change in yourself.

If you do this daily and commit to it, you'll really start feeling amazing every day. I recommend doing it at the same time, either in the morning or before you go to bed.

To make it a solid habit, a really good trick is to associate it with a habit you already have, so perhaps after brushing your teeth, meditate for ten minutes and then reward yourself.

The reward can be anything, I used to reward myself with vegan ice cream but you can see how that could easily get out of hand, so now instead I just make myself a tasty salad.

How Vegan Meals Can Tone Your Muscles And Give You A Healthier Body.

A whole bunch of vegan proteins can reduce your risk of cardiovascular disease, through improved cholesterol and blood pressure profiles. According to Doctor Bahee Van de Bor, most meat eaters have a higher rate of saturated fat intake, thereby increasing their chances of developing cardiovascular diseases.

Vegans are also said to have lower BMI than non-vegans; thereby reducing their risk of diabetes. This is an extremely great way of life for people who desire to lose weight while maintaining a healthy lifestyle.

But one needs to be careful in the pursuit of vegan weight loss, because if your vegan meals contain too much starchy food, it could cause you to gain more weight. Balance your vegan meals for a healthy body.

As a result of the high and varied intake of fruit and fresh vegetables by vegans, they tend to have fresher and healthier looking skin than the average non-vegan. Fruits and vegetables are high in essential antioxidants and vitamins which are the basis for good looking and healthier skin. Vitamin E and C helps neutralize skin damaging radicals, and fights against spots and wrinkles. Zinc, found in beans (a major ingredient in most vegan diets) has been discovered to have the ability to combat zits, decrease inflammation, and prevent pimples.

Vegans have good sources of vitamin D, which includes fortified fats, unsweetened soya drinks, as well as exposure to summer sunlight. This vitamin is responsible for the toning of the muscles, teeth, and bones, and also keeping them healthy.

Vitamin B12, which is included in several vegan meals such as yeast extract, unsweetened soya drinks, and breakfast cereals, helps in maintaining a healthier body and a healthier nervous system. Vegan diets also decrease the risk of consuming any potentially harmful fats from animals, as animal fats have are linked to a many diseases; ranging from cancer to diabetes.

Vegan dieting also lowers the mortality rate by two percent, as the risk of death is increased by a high caloric intake of animal proteins. In other words, the vegan diet helps you live longer. Amazing!

Exactly How Going Vegan Helps You Lose Weight.

The typical advice for weight loss is to eat less and exercise more. While this is true, I feel like it really is not specific enough in today's day and age. So here it is: Essentially a plant based diet is far less calorie dense than an animal based diet. This means that per gram of food, you're going to be consuming less calories.

Now consider if you replace all your meals on a daily basis with vegan foods, you're then going to be eating far less calories than normal. Not only that, but you'll be increasing your metabolic rate with all the healthy food you've taken in.

Going vegan is then a guaranteed way to lose weight and if you keep it up, you can lose a lot of weight in a short period of time. I would encourage you to download an app called MyFitnessPal, where you can track your calories and see how much you're taking in and even how much you're burning. You can also use it to find new Vegan foods and join vegan eating communities, where you can ask all your vegan related questions. Good stuff!

Can Being Vegan Help You Gain Weight and Muscle?

Yes, almost certainly. I would recommend reading this also if you want to lose weight, as it'll give you an idea of what foods to use in moderation. In this case, it is paramount that you focus on high calorie vegan foods, for example nuts.

Almonds and cashews in particular are high in healthy fats and can help you bulk up and gain weight. Mixed nuts are a good variety pack to get if you get bored of just nomming on cashews all day, which I'm certainly guilty of since they're so tasty.

Plant based oils are also very high in calories. Canola and coconut oil are pushing 900 calories per hundred grams, which can be an incredible weight gain tool combined with a salad or if used sparingly in a shake.

In addition, avocados have up to 320 calories and can be used in sandwiches, eaten with crackers or on their own.

How Going Vegan Affects Your State Of Mind and Massively Improves Mental Health

A lot of people have claimed that they are happier after adopting the vegan lifestyle. First, there is the satisfaction that comes with knowing that you have managed to protect the rights and freedom of animals, and because of that animals are experiencing less suffering by the day.

Then there is the benefit of a healthier lifestyle which leads to a healthier body and immune system, amazing looking skin, toned muscles, as well as stronger bones. The Vegan diet also allows for the exploration of other dishes that you usually might not have tried if you had been a non-vegan.

The vegan lifestyle decreases your mortality rate and reduces the risk of you having heart disease or some forms of cancer that may be caused by consuming animal products. Going Vegan as a whole has succeeded in turning a lot of people into better humans; empathetic and kind to not only animals, but other people as well.

Saving others makes you happier with yourself and those around you. And that alone is enough reason to become vegan. The amazing thing about going vegan is that there is no cost involved in making the decision to take on the lifestyle, but the value that you get from being vegan is infinite. For most people, the vegan diet has become the only way of life and the best way they know how to live.

Save animals today by choosing Vegan as your way of life, while at the same time benefiting your body and your community.

Authors Note: Hey, I really hope you're enjoying the book so far. If you are, be sure to leave an honest review on Amazon. It would mean a lot to me and it'll help me write even better books in the future.

Chapter 3 – Vegan Recipes That Will Blow Your Mind

The Most Delicious Quick & Easy Vegan Recipes

Choosing what to do with your vegan ingredients is not as tricky as you think. There are a lot of easy and delicious recipes that can be made from your average vegan ingredients that you have lying around. You will not have to repeat meals again if you know about them, remember, it's all about practice. The more recipes you learn about and learn to cook, the more varied your cuisine as a vegan can be.

Spicy Curried Lentils

This dish is not only delicious, but it is filled with spices and vegetables that could serve as an amazing dish on a cold day.

Required Ingredients:

1 can of tomato paste.

2 garlic cloves.

3 cans of large of cauliflower floret.

1 can of frozen peas.

Basmati rice(cooked).

A three quarter can of chopped, shelled, and unsalted pistachios.

Black pepper.

Salt.

2 teaspoons of ground cumin.

2 medium shallots.

1 piece of jalapeno chilli.

2 teaspoons of ground coriander.

1 tablespoon of freshly squeezed lime juice.

1 can of coconut milk.

1 and a half cans of lentils.

4 slices of peeled fresh ginger.

2 cans of vegetable broth.

Method Of Preparation:

1. The first step is to pour all the cumin, jalapeno chilli, coriander, tomato paste, salt, black pepper, ginger, garlic, and pulse shallot into a food processor. Then, process this mixture until it's smooth, before transferring the ingredients to a seven or eight quarts slow-cooker bowl.

2. The coconut milk, lentils, a cup of water and vegetable broth should be added to the same mixture, with the cauliflower going on the top. The mixture should be allowed to cook on a high temperature for about five hours until the lentils become soft.

3. While your mixture is still cooking, add your peas, lime juice and salt. Serve with your cooked Basmati rice and garnish with pistachios.

Avocado, Beetroot, And Mushroom Salad

There is nothing quite as healthy as a salad. It's filled with countless vitamins and minerals and is easy to prepare. Avocado, Beetroot, and Mushroom salad is a perfect meal for making any vegans day!

Required ingredients:

2 ripe avocados.

3 tablespoons of olive oil.

A quarter can of lemon juice.

5 oz. baby kale.

8 oz. of chopped precooked beetroot.

4 medium Portobello mushroom caps.

2 sheets of crushed matzo.

Method Of Preparation:

1. Spray your Portobello mushroom caps with non-stick cooking spray, and add sprinkle of salt to a large baking sheet.

2. Roast your caps at a temperature of about 450 degrees Fahrenheit (230 degrees celsius), for about 20 minutes or until they become tender.

3. Whisk your lemon juice with a teaspoon of salt, olive oil and a teaspoon of pepper. Add your baby kale and beetroot.

4. Top with sliced avocados, matzo, and portobello mushroom caps.

5. Serve with the remaining dressing on the side.

Sweet Potato Soup

This serves both as a delicious soup and a curry sauce when made a bit thicker, with fresh vegetables. This can be served with white or brown rice.

Required Ingredients:

1 diced onion.

1 teaspoon of salt.

1 litre of vegan stock.

Lime juice from a single lime.

1 tablespoon of Vegan Thai curry paste.

2 teaspoons of vegetable oil.

400ml of reduced fat coconut milk (canned).

1 tablespoon of finely chopped fresh ginger.

1 oz. of finely chopped fresh coriander(as a garnish).

Method Of Preparation:

1. Oil should be added in a large, heavy base saucepan and placed on a medium-high heat stove.

2. Add your ginger and onion, and then stir for about five minutes or until your ingredients get soft.

3. Add curry paste and salt, and stir for three more minutes.

4. Add your coconut milk, sweet potato, and stock. Let it boil under reduced heat for about twenty minutes(Do not cover the pan).

5. Pour the soup in a blender or food processor and blend/process it.

5. Place the soup back on the heat and let it simmer.

6. Stir it in lime juice right before you serve.

7. Garnish with coriander and serve hot.

Carrot And Almond Spread

This goes perfectly with some crackers or dipped into with some veggie chips as a quick, delicious snack.

Required Ingredients:

Salt and pepper or vegetable broth to taste.

140 grams of carrots.

140 grams of activated almonds.

Method Of Preparation:

1. Dice your carrots. Collect them and place them in a pan, and boil until they become soft.

2. Mash the cooked carrots in a bowl, you can use a mortar and pestle for this.

3. Add your almonds into the bowl of mashed carrots and mix well.

4. Add broth or salt and pepper to taste.

5. Dip in with your crackers and veggie chips!

Tofu Curry

Required Ingredients:

1 onion.

1 tin of coconut milk.

3 teaspoons of tomato puree.

1 stock cube in half a cup of water.

250 grams of firm tofu.

1 red pepper.

2 teaspoons of turmeric.

2 teaspoons of curry powder.

Method Of Preparation:

1. Slice your onions finely. Then, fry them in a saucepan until they turn brown.

2. Add your curry powder and turmeric and stir for about three minutes.

3. Cut the other vegetables finely. Then add them to the pan.

4. Add your coconut milk, stock, and tomato puree.

5. Finally, add your firm tofu and cook on high heat.

6. Serve when all vegetables are fully cooked and tender.

Paprika Rice

If you are in a hurry, this is definitely the dish for you(3-4 servings).

Required Ingredients:

2 tablespoons of oil.

1 onion.

2 cloves of finely chopped garlic.

A can of frozen peas.

170 grams of white rice.

A can of white beans.

A can of frozen beans.

350 ml of hot water and a stock cube.

Method Of Preparation:

1. Chop your onions and add to a pan with oil, begin at medium heat.

2. Add your beans, paprika, and garlic.

3. Add your rice and stir until the oil coats the rice.

4. Turn down the heat, cover the pan and allow it to cook for 15 minutes.

5. When the rice turns soft and fluffy, add peas and sweet corn and cook for another 15 minutes.

6. Serve hot.

Perfect Vegan Desserts.

There are a lot of delicious desserts that can be made from vegan ingredients. So, having a sweet tooth will not be a disadvantage for you. Trust me, you can be Vegan and enjoy your fair share of sweet treats.

The Best Vegan Brownies

Chocolate is a global sweetheart and vegans are no exception. Cocoa powder is put into great use for this dessert.

Required Ingredients:

20 grams of cocoa powder.

Three and a quarter teaspoons of baking powder.

50 grams of golden syrup.

120 grams of soy milk.

110 grams of plain flour.

10 grams of desiccated coconut.

15 drops of vanilla extract.

80 grams of brown sugar.

Method Of Preparation:

1. Preheat oven to 360 degrees Fahrenheit (180 degrees Celsius)

2. Sieve your flour, baking powder, and cocoa powder into a bowl.

3. Add your sugar, syrup, milk, coconut, and vanilla into a large bowl and whisk thoroughly.

4. Pour batter into a greased round pan that is approximately 8" (20 cm) long.

5. Bake for twenty minutes in the preheated oven.

6. Rotate the pan halfway through cooking time.

7. Pierce brownies with a toothpick to check if they are done(If they are done, the tooth pick will come out dry).

Vegan Berry Muffins

This dessert is absolutely heavenly. It's not just nice, but packed with nutritious berries for added taste.

Required ingredients:

1 and a three quarts cup of self-rising flour.

A teaspoon of vanilla beans.

A two-quarter cup of soy milk.

A cup of mixed berries.

160 grams of hard coconut oil.

Three and a quarter cup of date paste.

Two flax eggs.

Method Of Preparation:

1. First of all, pre heat your oven to 360 degrees Fahrenheit (180 degrees celsius).

2. Prepare a cupcake tin with 12 medium cupcake wrappers.

3. Use an electric whisk in a medium sized bowl and whisk your coconut oil until it becomes smooth.

4. Add your date paste and whisk thoroughly for about two minutes.

5. Mix in your vanilla beans and flax eggs until your mixture is smooth.

6. Add in your flour and soy milk to the mixture, and fold it into the mixture.

7. Pour it into the cup cake wrappers.

8. Bake for approximately twenty five minutes until the cupcakes are firm and have risen well.

9. Serve. You can ice them before serving if you wish.

Lemon Cake

This cake is nutritious, delicious, and has a beautiful taste and smell that will linger even after you're done eating it all.

Required Ingredients:

200 grams of sugar.

Half teaspoon of Xanthan gum.

30 grams of soya flour.

250 grams of vegan margarine.

150 grams of plain flour.

15 grams of baking powder.

2 teaspoons of vanilla sugar.

200 ml of warm water mixed with the juices of two lemons.

100 grams of corn flour.

50 grams of almonds.

Finely grated zest of 2 lemons (use the ones from before).

Method Of Preparation:

1. Preheat your oven to 340 degrees Fahrenheit (170 degrees Celsius)

2. Line a cake loaf tin of about 12" (30 cm) and grease lightly.

3. Pour in your soya flour, sugar, vanilla sugar, vegan margarine, and xanthan gum into a large mixing bowl.

4. Mix the ingredients at low speed so you can check the consistency of the mixture.

5. Top your lemon juice with the warm water to a total of 200ml.

6. Mix the liquid with the mixture on a medium speed of about 3 to 4 minutes.

7. Sieve your corn flour, with the plain flour and baking powder into the mixture and fold with a spatula.

8. Pour it into the cake loaf tin and bake for about 60 to 75 minutes.

Follow Up: Icing For The Lemon Cake -

Required Ingredients:

3 tablespoons of lemon juice.

150 grams of icing sugar.

2 teaspoons of lemon zest.

Method Of Preparation:

1. Mix all the ingredients together and spread over your lemon cake.

Chapter 4 – Vegan Recipes for Kids & Toddlers

Vegan Dishes For Kids And Toddlers.

Children raised vegan can get their required nutrients with the right dishes. There are a lot of nutritious and tasty vegan dishes for your babies and your toddlers. Here are a few:

Bean Stew

This is an amazing source of protein.

Required Ingredients:

1 diced carrot.

1 dsp of dried lentils.

A small diced parsnip.

A half teaspoon of mixed herbs.

15 grams of flour.

Vegetable oil required for frying.

A dsp of tomato puree.

A small finely chopped onion.

A half litre of vegetable stock.

75 grams of dried beans and peas soaked overnight.

Method Of Preparation:

1. Start by lightly frying your onions in the vegetable oil.

2. Add all the remaining ingredients except the flour.

3. Allow it to boil and simmer gently for about an hour, so the vegetables can cook properly.

4. Add a tablespoon of cold water to your flour and mix gently into your paste.

5. Allow it to stew and cook for some minutes till it thickens.

6. Add the puree or serve it that way if the child is still a toddler.

Fruit Tofu Dessert

The lovely taste of fruits and cream is a favourite of little kids. It is easy to make and eat.

Required Ingredients:

75 grams of silken tofu.

50 grams of live soya yoghurt.

75 grams of mixed dried fruits.

Method Of Preparation:

1. Cook your dried fruits in a little water gently until they become soft.

2. Cool the dried fruits for a small amount of time.

3. Add your silken tofu and yoghurt to the fruits and blend until your mixture becomes smooth and creamy.

Quick Rusks

Babies absolutely love chewing on these, especially when they start teething. This dish is suitable for babies that are 10 months and above.

Required Ingredients:

A thick slice from a loaf of wholemeal bread (ezekiel bread is recommended).

Method Of Preparation:

1.Cut your bread into thick strips.

2. Place your cut bread on a baking tray.

3. Bake for about 15 minutes at a temperature of 350 degrees or gas mark four.

4: Remove and serve to your toddlers.

Plain Fruit Jelly

This little darling is just perfect to give to your kid as a take-away meal, especially to take to a party with other kids.

Required Ingredients:

2 heaped teaspoons of agar-agar powder.

Soya cream.

500 ml to 750 ml of sweet fruit juice(It can be any fruit of your choice).

Method Of Preparation:

1. Heat your fruit juice till it boils.

2. Add the agar-agar powder and allow it to cook for about 2 to 3 minutes.

3. Pour into a jelly mound and allow it to set in a fridge overnight.

4. Serve with the Soya cream.

Baby Muesli

This is a perfect breakfast for your growing child.

Required ingredients:

5 pieces of dried apricot(Simmered in water until it gets soft).

150 ml of fortified soya milk.

1 pear(peeled and chopped).

15 grams of oats.

Method Of Preparation:

1. Put your oats and soya milk in a saucepan.

2. Simmer the ingredients for about two or three minutes, until the mixture thickens.

3. Cool it a little after removing it from the fire.

4. Add the cooked apricots and pear chunks and blend until it gets smooth and creamy.

Minestrone Soup

This should be made nice and thick. It is suitable for kids aged 10 months and above.

Required Ingredients:

1 litre of vegetable stock.

A medium carrot.

Half a stick of celery.

A medium potato.

Half crushed clove garlic.

Vegetable oil.

One chopped small onion.

A small tin of haricot beans.

75 grams of dried pasta shapes.

Half large chopped tin tomatoes.

50 grams of peas.

50 grams of finely chopped cabbage.

Method Of Preparation:

1. Fry your onion, garlic, and celery in a pan with your vegetable oil.

2. Add the other ingredients except the pasta and simmer for approximately twenty minutes.

3. Add your pasta and simmer again for about ten minutes. Done.

Chapter 5 – The Most Incredible Vegan Sandwiches, Snacks and Salads

If, like me, you live a busy lifestyle, these Vegan sandwiches and snacks will be absolutely ideal for you. Make sure you choose the right kind of bread, I would recommend ezekiel bread or sourdough bread. These breads are not only yummy, but high in protein. In some recipes I do recommend the kinds of bread I like to have, in this case you can replace them with your bread preference. I would recommend trying a few of the below recipes and seeing which ones work for you.

Bloody Mary

This is a nice and easy combination of black pepper, sun dried tomato paste, tomatoes, and salt on an olive ciabatta. Yummy!

Required Ingredients:

Black pepper

Sun dried tomato paste

Tomatoes

Salt

Olive Ciabatta Roll

Method of Preparation:

1: Simply slice your tomatoes into fairly thick segments.

2: Apply the sun dried tomato paste onto the olive ciabatta bread.

3: Arrange the tomatoes on top of the sun dried paste, sprinkle salt and black pepper.

4: Cut into two halves and enjoy!.

Chickpea Craving

This tasty chickpea based dish requires less than 15 minutes to prepare but has taste that'll leave you craving more for hours. The best part is, there's no chick involved at all.

Required Ingredients:

1-2 cups chickpeas

Teaspoon of Lemon juice

One tomato

Cumin

Tahini

Method of Preparation:

1: Simply slice your tomato, this time into fairly thin slices.

2: Get a large bowl and mix the chick peas with the lemon juice.

3: When the chickpeas are adequately covered add your cumin and tahini.

4: This can be served with rice or used as a delicious sandwich filling.

Chocoholic

This is for the chocolate loving vegans out there. I would put the taste of this one somewhere on the scale of incredible to Vegan Heaven. It is simply made from chocolate spread, hazelnut, and bananas. The heavenly taste is sure to keep you craving more.

Required Ingredients:

A Vegan Chocolate spread

Lemon syrup

A banana

Strawberries (optional)

Method of Preparation

1: Slice up your banana. Make sure it's adequately ripe.

2: Spread the chocolate onto the bottom of the sandwich, making sure you don't put too much.

3: Place the bananas on top of the chocolate spread and drizzle your lemon syrup on top. You can also add strawberries if you like to combine these flavours.

4: Enjoy!

Greek Groove

This sandwich is the authentic taste of Greece without even having to travel! It's easy to prepare and delicious and will make you feel like you've spent an evening under the Greek sun looking out over a pristine beach.

Required Ingredients:

Vegan Dairy Free Greek Style Cheese

Fresh Basil

One tomato

Olive oil

One red onion

Of course, olives.

Method of Preparation:

1: Dice the Vegan mock feta such that you've got squishable little cubes of flavour.

2: Cut your tomato into thick slices and prepare an amount of basil you like.

3: Prepare your red onion also. You want fairly thick slices here as well for maximum flavour.

4: You can cut your olives into pieces, if you've bought ones with seeds in them I recommend deseeding them at this point. Otherwise, you can just use your whole olives.

5: Line the bottom of the sandwich with your sliced tomatoes, put your feta cheese on top. Follow with your red onion and olives, top with basil and sprinkle a bit of olive oil.

Mock Duck

If you're craving some oriental cuisine, this sandwich will certainly satisfy you. This is definitely one of the more exotic Vegan dishes I've prepared and it is certainly exotic in its taste as well.

This delicious meal with a really weird name is made up of bean sauce, spring onions, black bean sauce, bean sprouts, and shredded Chinese leaves. It is definitely a name and taste to remember.

Required Ingredients:

One spring onion

Black bean sauce

Bean sprouts

Shredded Chinese leaves

Method of Preparation:

1: Prepare your spring onion, I like to give mine a good old wash before dicing it.

2: Cover the bottom of the sandwich in your prepared bean sprouts.

3: Place your spring onion segments on top with the shredded chinese leaves.

4: Cover with black bean sauce to taste.

Pizza Di Action

Well, who doesn't love pizza? The dish is just as promising as its name. You know what's even better than regular pizza? Vegan pizza. Need I say more?

Required Ingredients:

Sun dried tomato paste

Vegan pepperoni (Typically quorn)

One red pepper

Oregano

One onion

Vegan Dairy Free Cheese (Optional)

Method of Preparation:

1: Cover the base of your sandwich with your sun dried tomato paste.

2: The next layer is your vegan pepperoni, add as much as you'd like.

3: Cut up your red pepper and onion and place the segments upon the pepperoni.

4: Cover in oregano to taste.

5: As an optional step, you can add your favourite vegan cheese as well.

6: I'd recommend toasting this particular sandwich for maximum flavour.

Illustrious Indian

An authentic taste of India. This is a quick and easy dish to make if you buy the onion bhaji beforehand, but you can also make it yourself. This dish is quite easy to make and contains onion bhaji with tahini sauce, and salad in pitta bread.

Required Ingredients:

Onion bhaji (premade or your own)

Tahini sauce

Pitta bread

Your choice of salad

Method of Preparation:

1: Put your onion bhaji inside of your pitta bread, being careful not to cause the bread to split open. I recommend cutting up the onion bhaji beforehand.

2: Add your salad, and then the tahini sauce on top of that.

Sweet Peanut

Almost certainly a dream come true for any and all peanut lovers. This delectable combination of peanut butter, raisins, cinnamon and carrots provides the perfect snack for any occasion.

Required Ingredients:

Peanut Buter

California Raisins

Cinnamon

Diced carrots

Method of Preparation:

1: I would recommend using Whole Meal Bread for this one. Simply use your peanut butter as a base, with the carrots layered on top.

2: Secondly, sprinkle raisins to taste on the carrot layer and top with a very slight, but purposeful amount of cinnamon.

Wee Willie Winkie

Okay let me be honest. It's a Vegan hot dog, but with a slight twist. Try it for yourself and I bet it's more delicious than any regular hot dog you've ever tried. You can make this one hot, or cold, but I'd definitely recommend it hot.

Required Ingredients:

Vegan sausage bun

Vegan sausages

Black beans

Lettuce

HP Sauce

Method of Preparation:

1: Line the vegan sausage bun with your dried black beans.

2: Stuff the remaining area with lettuce, but not too much. Leave space for the vegan sausage.

3: Place the vegan sausage hot from the oven (homemade) or cold on top of the lettuce bed made for it.

4: Cover in HP sauce or a vegan sauce of your choice.

5: Enjoy your delicious hotdog substitute.

Bubble 'n' Squeak

This is one of the most interesting sandwiches I've ever eaten. With a mix of flavours, it's sure to be a culinary experience that keeps you on your toes.

Required Ingredients:

Shredded baked potato

Vegan mayo

Lightly sautéed shredded green cabbage and onions

Toasted sesame seeds

Sea salt

Black pepper

Method of Preparation:

1: The first layer of your sandwich will involve the shredded baked potato. Remember, it should be shredded finely, so that there is space for your other ingredients.

2: Top with your shredded green cabbage and onions, then sprinkle toasted sesame seeds.

3: Cover with your desired amount of vegan mayo.

4: Sprinke sea salt and black pepper to taste.

Cinderella Surprise

Find your own glass slipper with this tropical mix of everything Vegan. Just like the Pumpkin carriage, the taste of this sandwich is certain to carry you to your own personal Vegan fairytale.

Required Ingredients:

Toasted pumpkin

Red pepper

Coriander seeds

Raisins

Chillies

Grated carrots

Red onions

Orange Zest

Method of preparation:

1: Your toasted pumpkin will be the base of your sandwich, followed by your red peppers and red onions.

2: Your scond layer consists of your grated carrots, and your orange zest for the tangy middle.

3: Top with raisins and coriander seeds, as well as sprinkling a few chillies if you are a fan of spice.

4: Enjoy this delicious sandwich, straight out of a fairytale.

Cocktail Cob

This is what corn is supposed to taste like. The ultimate Vegan corn experience is right here. A delightful mix of tofu and a Vegan prawn cocktail dressing.

Required Ingredients:

Tin of sweet corn

Strips of smoked tofu

Lettuce

Nori flakes

A prawn cocktail dressing, made of:

Lime juice

Salt

Tomato sauce

Mustard

Vegan mayo

1: Mix the dressing in a large bowl until its consistency is fairly thick.

2: Line your sandwich with your smoked tofu strips and cover in sweet corn.

3: Put your lettuce on top and sprinkle nori flakes on top of that.

4: Cover in your homemade Vegan prawn cocktail dressing.

Eggless Salad

Salad is the quintessential Vegan dish, however this salad has a bit of a twist to it. Using spring onion with a mix of vegan mayo, sweet corn and cress, this is a taste to remember with no eggs required.

Required Ingredients:

Diced spring onion

Homemade scrambled tofu

Sweet corn

Shredded cress

Vegan mayo

1: Simply acquire a large bowl and place your shredded cress, sweet onion and scrambled tofu first. Mix slightly

2: Add your sweet corn and vegan mayo to taste.

3: A vegan salad dressing of your choice in this situation is the metaphorical icing on the cake.

4: This can be used as a sandwich filling if you'd like as well.

Korma Have A Go

This sandwich is quite the roller coaster. One you might be initially wary of, but if you have a go your taste buds will bless you afterwards.

Required Ingredients:

Crispy lettuce

Homemade smoked tofu or vegan chicken substitute

Curried vegan mayonnaise

1: Use your vegan chicken or homemade smoked tofu as the base of the sandwich.

2: Shred your crispy lettuce, topping your other ingredients and finish with curried vegan mayonnaise.

Moussaka Me Gently

A creative, mediteranian style Vegan dish.

Required Ingredients:

Vegan cheese

Nutmeg

Roasted Aubergine

Sundried Tomato paste

Garlic

Creamed Potato

Method of Preparation:

1: Your sandwich base will consist of your sundried tomato paste topped with your roasted aubergine.

2: Add your creamed potato and nutmeg as your second layer.

3: Grate your vegan cheese as a tasty topping and add garlic as you please.

Que? Quesadilla?

This Mexican Meat-free Marvel is almost certain to blow your mind. That's right a fully Vegan quesadilla.

Required Ingredients:

Two tortillas

Thinly sliced vegan cheese

Thiny sliced tomatoes

Salad of your choice

1: Take your two tortillas and place your thinly sliced vegan cheese and tomatoes between them.

2: Toast your sandwich up on both sides of a dry frying pan.

3: Cut the sandwich into quarters and serve with a salad of your choice.

4: Enjoy the texture of the melted cheese and soft tomato in this delicious Vegan quesadilla.

Conclusion

Thank you again for downloading this book!

I hope this book was able to help you to on your Vegan Diet Journey!

The next step is to take action on all the steps in this book! Share this book with all your friends and family if you found it helpful, let's speed up the Vegan Revolution!

Finally, if you enjoyed this book, then I'd like to ask you for a favor, would you be kind enough to leave a review for this book on Amazon? It'd be greatly appreciated!

Click here to leave a review for this book on Amazon!

Thank you and good luck!

Manufactured by Amazon.ca
Bolton, ON